The Snot that Animals Have Got

by Paul Mason and
Tony De Saulles

WAYLAND
www.waylandbooks.co.uk

First published in Great Britain in 2021 by Wayland

Editor: Melanie Palmer
Designer: Peter Scoulding
Picture researcher: Diana Morris

HB ISBN: 978 1 5263 1709 4
PB ISBN: 978 1 5263 1710 0
Ebook ISBN: 978 1 5263 1898 5

An imprint of
Hachette Children's Group
Part of Hodder & Stoughton
Carmelite House
50 Victoria Embankment
London EC4Y 0DZ

An Hachette UK Company
www.hachette.co.uk
www.hachettechildrens.co.uk

Printed in China

Picture credits:
Nature PL: Nick Upton 25t.Shutterstock: Acceptphoto 25c; Birkir Asgeirsson 9tr; Robert Avgustin 7t; Buttchi 3 Sha Life 18c; Rich Carey 25b; Chokasawatdikorn 14t; B Costelloe 7c; Robert Eastman 11bc; Dirk Ercken 4ca; Shane Gross 20b;Kirk Holger 15t; Irina K 11bl; Irin-k 4b; Cathy Keifer 15c; Arzu Kerimli 13t; Tomasz Klejdysz 19br;Kletr 25c; Rita Kochmarjova 26b; Holly Kuchera 11br; Anna Kucherova 21b;LimetimeStock 15b; Lizard 24t; Maikbrand 13br; Richard A McMillin 13bl; Kyla Metzker 4t; Nosyrevy 4c; LeonP 8bl; Peapop 23b; Oksana Perkins 17b;Dmitry Petlin 11c; Olly Plu 22t; Dr Morely Read 10b; Schankz 16t;Natalia Silatovskaia 28t; Mathias Sunke 9tl; Tristan Tan 26t; Uzuri 8t.

Contents

What is SNOT?

Snot is also called mucus. (There are other, less-polite names for it, too.) Snot is one of the most useful things around.

Animals use snotty mucus in lots of ways: to catch their dinner, repel attacks by predators, send messages and eat tricky food.

What do you think these animals use snot for? (Find out if you were right on page 30.)

1 Slimy salamander.

2 Poison dart frog.

3 Goby fish

4 Ladybird

Recipe for Snot

Snot is about 95% water. It also contains things called mucins (which is said: 'mew-sins'). These mucins are what makes snot gooey and slimy.

BELIEVE IT OR SNOT!

Spit (scientific name: saliva) contains snot. Like snot, spit is mostly water, but it also contains mucus and other chemicals.

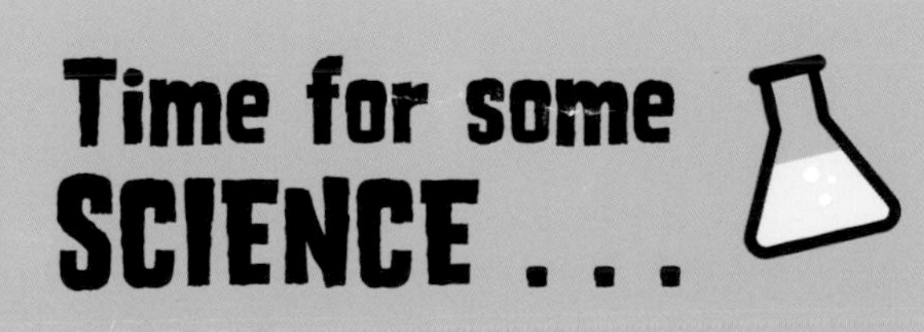

Why is mucus sticky?

It's because mucins have a negative electrical charge. This attracts other substances. Imagine tomato sauce sticking to spaghetti: it works a bit like that.

The SNOT you have got!

You produce extra mucus when you're ill.

Humans are animals too – and snot is SO useful to us humans that we normally produce about four cupfuls a day.

Look for the snotty lining

Your nose, throat and guts are all lined with mucus. Elsewhere in your body, slippery mucus stops bits of you squeaking against each other when you move.

Without mucus, we could not move smoothly.

Nose protection

We all know that snot and noses go together. Nose snot stops things like pollen and dirt being breathed into your body. They get trapped in the snot.

I'm stuck

No way through!

Booger picking

After it's been there a while, nose snot dries out and turns into a booger. Among humans, picking out boogers is considered impolite. This is not so in the animal world: plenty of animals – particularly apes – pick their boogers.

When animals pick out dry boogers, it helps keep their noses moist. They can smell food or threats more easily.

Mucus helps destroy bacteria or viruses that we breathe in. They get stuck to mucus in the nose and throat, preventing them from reaching the lungs. Some germs get expelled as snot, others are swallowed in the mucus and destroyed by stomach acid.

Animal nose BLOWERS

You might think humans are the only animals that blow their noses – but you'd be wrong. There are plenty of animals with special techniques for clearing out unwanted snot.

Monkey business

Monkeys and gorillas often blow their noses: it helps them smell better. Gorillas often pick snot out with their fingers, then taste (or eat) it. If that sounds disgusting, wait until you hear about bonobo monkeys ...

When bonobo mothers see that their baby is a bit snotty, they bend down and ... suck out the snot with their MOUTHS. Yuk!

SQUELCH!

Capuchin monkeys sometimes use twigs to pick their noses.

Drip-and-lickers

Animals without hands need another way to clear out unwanted nose dribble. Fortunately, many of them are equipped with the perfect wiper-upper: a tongue. Cows, giraffes and dogs all use their tongues for snot clearance.

Dogs use their tongues for all kinds of jobs.

Ready ... aim ... SNOT!

Animals have all kinds of uses for snotty fluids – including as a weapon. Some can even fire the fluid at their enemies.

Sticky liquid stops the attacker from moving.

Glue-gun termites

Some North American termites can fire a sticky, snot-like liquid out of the top of their head. Despite being blind, the termites can hit targets several centimetres away.

Sniper worms

Velvet worms are the snipers of the worm world. They fire snotty, gluey liquid from their head at their prey. The prey is trapped in the liquid, then eaten.

Velvet worms hunt in packs led by a big, fierce female.

Stinky Snotters

Some geckos can fire snotty fluid out of a gland in their tails. The fluid smells pretty terrible and sticks to whatever it hits. It puts off predators in a similar way to a skunk's spray.

I wouldn't, if I were you.

These geckos can fire stinky liquid over a metre – and they're good shots.

No, he's right – DON'T.

Opossums can do a similar trick with mucus from their bottoms. They can't fire it at anyone, though. It just oozes out and smells so bad that it puts off predators.

OOZE! OOZE!

Oh, yuew, yuk!

Oh Mum, don't let me smell any more!

Jelly SNOTTERS

BELIEVE IT OR SNOT!

There really is a thing called 'sea snot', a layer of mucus that sometimes appears on the surface of the sea. Scientists are not sure why this happens.

So many sea creatures use mucus that it's amazing we don't come out of the sea after a swim covered in slime. In the water world of snot though, the jellyfish rules.

Jellyfish glue

Jellyfish have a layer of sticky mucus over their stingers. It's there to act as glue. Once the prey has been stung, the mucus stops it escaping before it can be moved to the jellyfish's mouth.

On some jellyfish, mucus with stingers in it washes off into the water – making it possible to be stung by a jellyfish that's not even there.

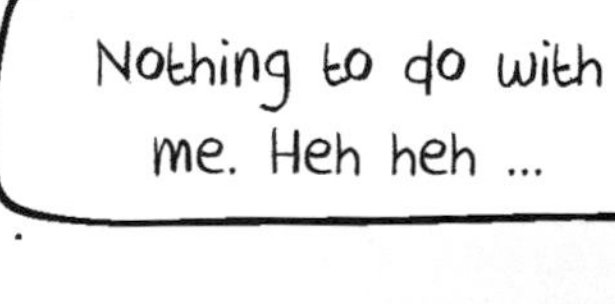

Time for some SCIENCE . . .

Jellyfish are about 95 per cent water. Most jellyfish bodies have three main parts:

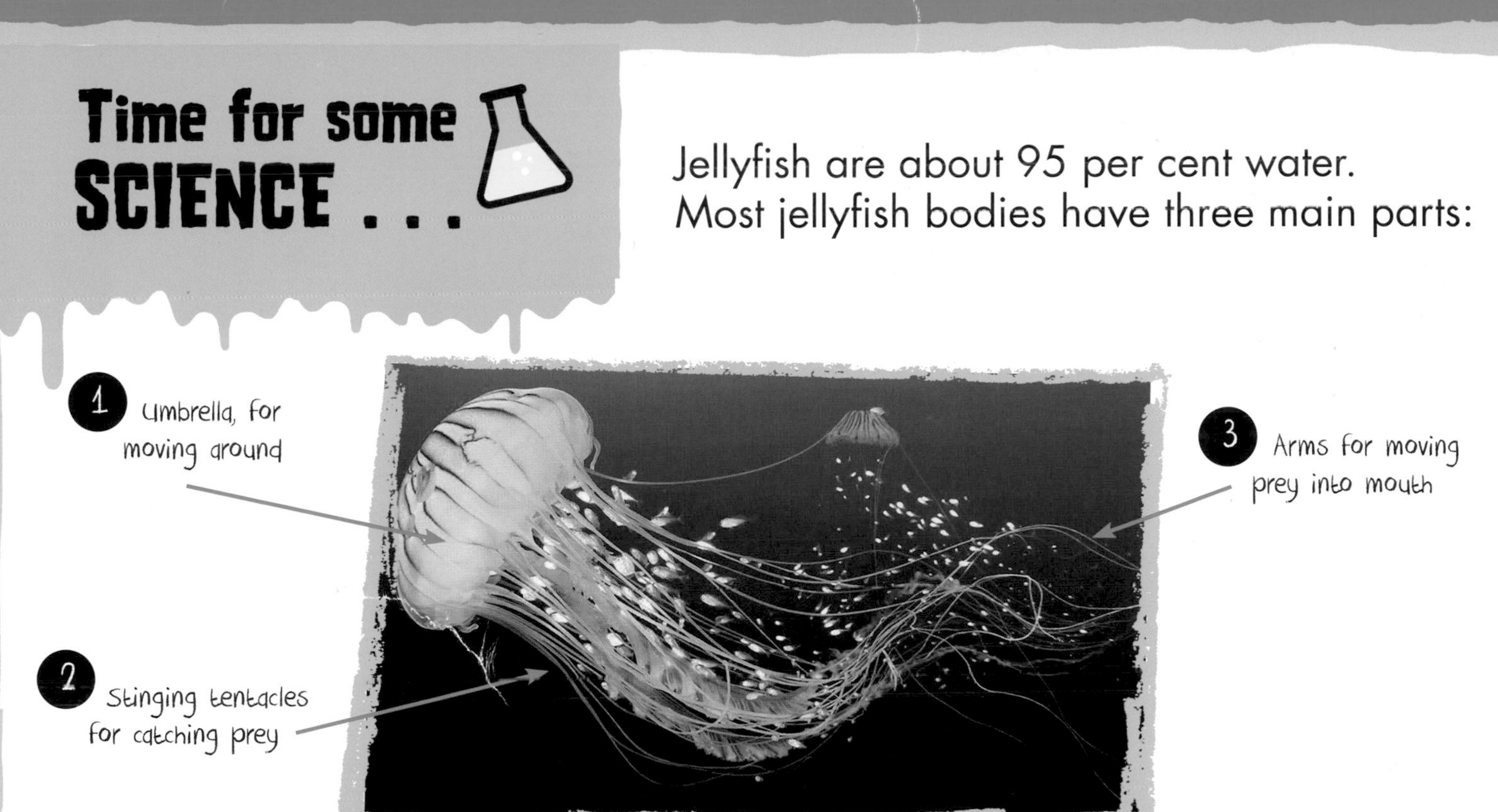

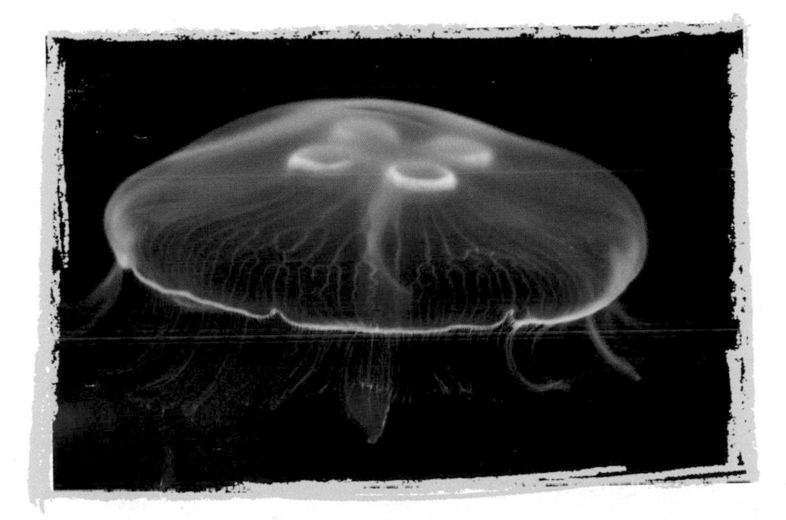

Moon jellyfish catch food using gluey mucus on their undersides. The prey gets stuck, then gets eaten.

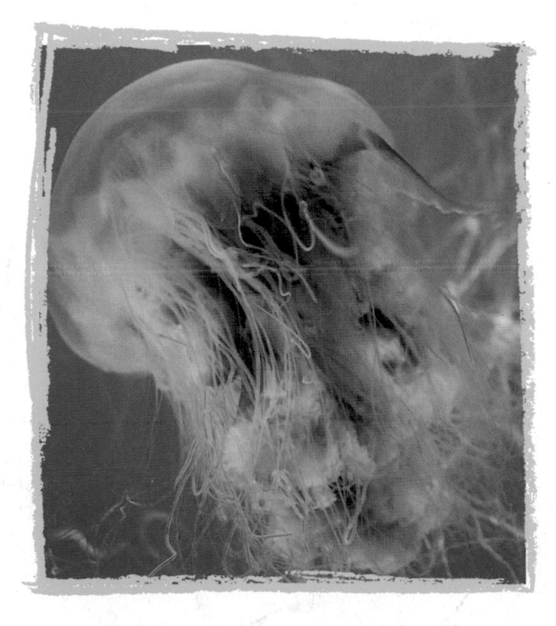

Lion's mane jellyfish make SO much mucus that they are sometimes called 'snotties'.

SNOTTY hunters!

Some animal predators have found ways to use snotty mucus for hunting. They turn it into anything from fishing nets to sticky lassos.

Fishing with snot

Some sea snails, worms and creatures called larvaceans use snot as a kind of fishing net. They eat tiny ocean plants, and sticky mucus is a great way to capture these. The only problem is, the animals sometimes have to eat their own snot, too, because the food is stuck to it.

Comb jellies are not actually jellyfish, even though they look very similar.

Some comb jellies use snot to catch food in a different way. They lasso their prey with sticky strings of it, filled with stingers. Then the comb jelly pulls in its victim to be eaten.

Sticky tongues

Frogs, toads and chameleons all use mucus to catch food. Their long tongues are coated with a sticky mucus. When they see a tasty insect, the tongue flicks out and grabs it, then whizzes back in. Gulp!

SNOT (and spit) medicine

Our bodies sometimes produce extra snot – when we have a cold, for example. And we're not the only animals with health-related uses for snot.

OW!

LICK!

LICK!

LICK!

'Lick your wounds' means 'try to recover from an injury'. The expression probably came from watching animals.

Snot and spit

Sometimes the snot is mixed in with spit. Dogs, cats, rodents, horses, monkeys and gorillas, for example, use spit as a kind of medicine. They lick wounds to help them heal.

Time for some SCIENCE . . .

Animals lick their wounds because their saliva contains special chemicals. These help blood to clot and stop infections.

Snot health check

How do you give a whale a health check? You use their snot, that's how. When whales surface, snotty stuff comes firing out of their blowholes. Scientists can find out lots of information from it: for example, whether the whale is healthy, pregnant or stressed.

To gather whale snot, scientists have built a drone called SnotBot. The SnotBot hovers above the whale – and when it surfaces it grabs a load of snot.

SNOTTY defences

Some animals use the slippery qualities of mucus as a defence – like a slippery fish, sliding out of a fisherman's grip. But there are other ways to defend yourself with snot.

Hagfish live in cold, deep waters around the world.

World's snottiest fish

The hagfish lives in the deep sea, where it eats carrion. When threatened, it releases huge amounts of slimy snot from the sides of its body. The snot is held together by long, strong, silk-like fibres. The hagfish is aiming to clog up an attacker's gills, so that it cannot breathe.

Snotty ink

Lobsters love to snack on a type of snail called a sea hare. When a lobster approaches, the sea hares release snotty mucus, mixed with purple ink. The mucus seems to act as a cloak of chemical invisibility, fooling the lobster into thinking the sea hare has disappeared.

I'm SURE I saw something!

Snotty botty bubbles

Froghoppers are tiny insects that can leap huge distances when threatened. They are sometimes called spittlebugs. Froghopper nymphs hide from danger by bubbling frothy mucus from their bottoms and covering themselves in it.

BELIEVE IT OR SNOT!

The froghopper's froth is called cuckoo spit, even though it has nothing to do with cuckoos.

SNOTTY sliders

Wet, snotty mucus is super slippery – just ask anyone who's tried to grab hold of an eel. Animals use this slipperiness in ways that might surprise you.

Speedy Snot

Barracuda are among the fastest fish in the sea. Their speed comes mainly from their long, powerful bodies and large tail fins – but the barracuda has a snotty trick to add a bit more speed ... Scales coated in slimy mucus.

50 kph? No problem.

Slippery Snot

Earthworms do not travel as fast as barracuda (even the quickest only reach about 0.73 kph). They use snot in a similar way, though. The earthworm's body is coated in slippery mucus, which helps it wriggle and dig its way through the soil.

Safety Snot

There is nothing a river otter likes to eat more than a nice, fresh fish. The trouble with fish, though, is that they are covered with rough, sharp scales.

So that they are not hurt as they swallow, the otters have extra-thick mucus lining their throats. It protects them from sharp fish scales.

SNOT glue

Snot can be slippery – but it can also act like a glue. Slugs and snails use this gluey snot to pull off all kinds of tricks.

Wall-climbing snails

How can a snail climb up a vertical wall, when it doesn't have hands or feet? The answer is: using snot. The snotty mucus that oozes out of a snail's underside acts as glue, holding the snail in place. It moves along on this gluey layer using muscles inside its foot.

Slug Superglue

If you're a slug, how do you stop birds just picking you up and eating you? The answer is: snot.

Time for some SCIENCE . . .

Some slug slime has now been found to be stronger than superglue. Even though it is strong, the glue is also flexible. Researchers are hoping to find ways of using slug slime to make a glue for people's hearts after they have been damaged.

Toxic SNOT

BELIEVE IT OR SNOT!

A snail's shell helps to keep it safe – but some snails have a second line of defence. Their mucus also smells and tastes revolting.

Snot can be an excellent way of defending yourself from danger – whether the snot is simply foul-tasting, or actually contains toxic chemicals.

Snotty gobies

Meet the fish that's so snotty that part of its scientific name is the Latin for snot: *Callogobius mucosus*, the sculptured goby.

The goby's mucus tastes REALLY bad – so bad that predators often swallow one, then spit it back out again.

Time for some SCIENCE . . .

Toxins are natural chemicals that harm other living things. They are usually either poisons or venoms:

- if something bites you and you die, it's venom
- if you eat something and die, it's poison.

Bootlace worms are coated in toxic mucus.

The mucus on a pufferfish's body contains toxins.

Dead, but still deadly

Lionfish are about 45 cm long, which is big enough to make a meal for a shark or ray ... but nothing eats the lionfish. It's just too toxic.

Even when it's dead, the lionfish is deadly. The only way to stop its spines being toxic is to heat them to a high temperature, for example by cooking them.

UH-OH.

Message in a DRIBBLE

Snot and spit are both used by animals to communicate. Eels, for example, use mucus to find out whether other eels are male or female, and how old they are.

Electric Eels

On the Snail-road

Snails often follow the mucus trails left behind by other snails. Travelling on these snail-roads makes moving easier – and could also lead the snail to food, or a mate.

Yum, lettuce!

Nom, nom!

Spit messages

Some animals, such as dogs, use spit, rather than snot, to pass on messages.

Dogs, wolves and other animals lick their young. The spit that's left behind is a way of recognising them later.

Some ants spit on their larvae. The spit carries chemicals that seem to affect whether the larvae become workers, soldiers or even a queen.

Termites (whose mounds are made partly of spit) also use spit to communicate. Whenever two termites meet, they exchange saliva as a way of swapping chemical messages. Important messages are conveyed via the queen.

Sunshine.

1

X-ray view of mound.

Mound gets too hot.

Messengers bring news to the queen.

2

3

Queen releases chemical message for workers.

4

The workers hurry deep into the mound, collect water, climb back up and coat the walls with water to cool it down.

Sleeping with SNOT

Snot can be slippery, gluey, poisonous, foul-tasting, a tasty snack, a hiding place ... animals even use it to make themselves somewhere to live.

Sandy house

How do you build a house of sand at the bottom of the sea? Using snot, of course. Some mantis shrimp line their burrows with snotty mucus, to stop them collapsing.

Coral reefs

Over a quarter of the world's different fish live near coral reefs. The reefs form when young corals find a good place to live ... then glue themselves in place using snotty mucus.

Nests of Spit

Lots of birds hold their nests together with spit, which contains gluey mucus. Young cave swiftlets, though, have to put up with more than just a BIT of spit. Their nests are made almost COMPLETELY of dried spit.

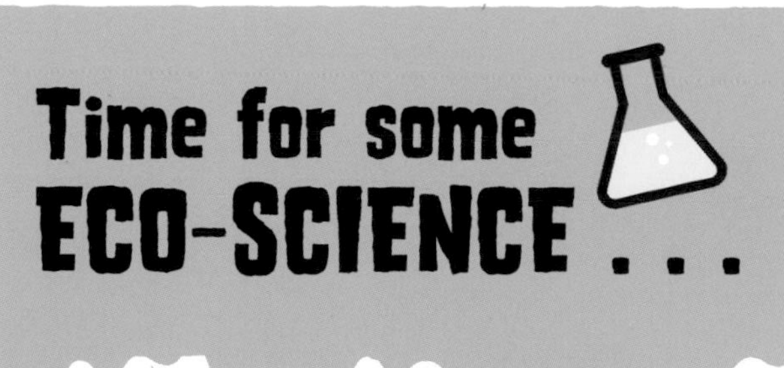

In Asia, cave swiftlet nests are cut down to be used in bird's-nest soup. Millions of nests each year are removed, and the number of cave swiftlets is falling as a result.

SNOTTY fast facts

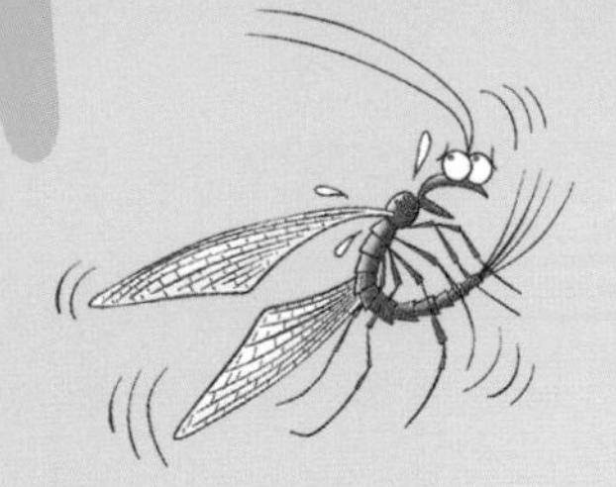

The California sheephead fish and some species of parrotfish seem to cloak themselves in mucus at night, as a way of avoiding detection by predators.

Fish, frogs, earthworms, catfish and corals all secrete mucus containing chemicals that protect them against bacteria and viruses.

The 'ink' that octopuses, squids and cuttlefish release when threatened is actually snotty mucus, mixed with a dark colour.

Animals as different as the Texas horned lizard and the clownfish use mucus to protect themselves from bites and stings.

Answers to page 4:

1) The slimy salamander breathes through its skin. Mucus keeps the skin damp and able to absorb maximum oxygen.

2) The poison dart frog lives in trees, but its tadpoles need water – so the frog sticks them to its back with mucus.

3) The goby fish has a protective layer of mucus instead of scales.

4) Ladybirds (like quite a lot of insects) use mucus to glue their eggs to leaves.

Glossary

bacteria tiny living creatures made up of just one cell

carrion dead flesh

clot a build-up of dried, hardened blood

corals tiny sea animals that live together and form coral reefs

drone small, unmanned flying craft

gill one of the openings on the side of a fish's head through which it breathes

gland part of an animal's body that releases special chemicals, either inside or outside the body

guts the long tube in your body, through which food passes

infection illness caused by something (for example, bacteria) getting inside the body

larva second stage in the development of most insects (the stages are usually egg, larva, pupa and adult)

mate animal to have young with

moist slightly wet

nymph second stage in the life of some insects (with these insects, the stages are egg, nymph and adult)

oxygen gas contained in air, which all animals need to breathe to stay alive

predator animal that hunts and kills others

pregnant carrying young that have not yet been born

prey animal that is hunted by others as food

repel push away or fight off

scales small plates of hard material that cover the skin of most fish

secrete leak or ooze out

sniper accurate shooter

toxic containing chemicals that harm other living things

virus tiny object that multiplies inside the cells of a living thing, damaging or destroying them

Index

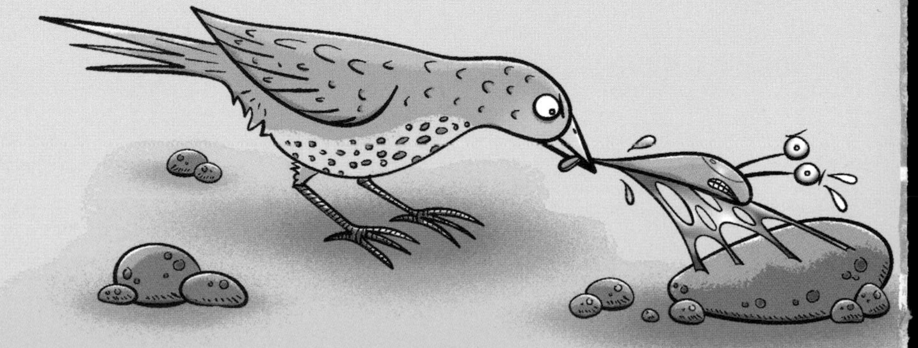